Table of Contents:

Introduction

Hawaii's Pacific Rim Cuisine finds inspiration from some of the greatest culinary traditions in the world. The Aloha Spice Company Seasonings & Rubs reflect the diversity of these cultures and flavors unique to Hawai'i.

We make our blends in small batches using the highest quality herbs and spices available. 'Alaea Sea Salt, known for its characteristic red color, is the traditional seasoning used by Hawaiians to flavor and preserve food. Found only in the Hawaiian Islands, we use 'alaea sea salt in most of our herb and spice blends.

This book contains some suggestions and recipes of how to use The Aloha Spice Company Seasonings & Rubs. Feel free to experiment and adapt our blends to your own recipes to add *"the flavor of Aloha"* to any dish!

For more information visit: www.alohaspice.com

Aloha Prime Steak

Seasoning & Rub

Aloha Prime Steak Seasoning & Rub

This seasoning is ideal for rubbing into all meats including lamb, chicken and duck. For a delicious prime rib roast, press a 1/4" thick layer of seasoning on the fat side of the roast before roasting in the oven. Rub on any cut of steak before grilling or apply to rotisserie of leg of lamb where the orange peel and coriander accents the richness of the meat. A simple filet mignon soars with this seasoning!

Grilled Steak with Roasted Red Potatoes
(serves 2)

2 – 8 oz. steak (New York or other prime cut)
4 Tbsp. Aloha Prime Steak Seasoning & Rub

Serve with
4 red potatoes or other small potato, quartered
1 large carrot, peeled and cut into 2" pieces
2 tomatoes, halved across the equator
6 Tbsp. olive oil
2 Tbsp. parsley, chopped for garnish

Instructions for Grilled Steak with Roasted Red Potatoes

Preparing the Vegetables

Toss the potatoes and carrots with 4 Tbsp. of the olive oil, coating thoroughly. Lay out in a single layer on a sheet pan. Season with salt and pepper (if desired). Roast in oven at 350° for 40 minutes until brown & tender. Place tomatoes on tray in oven, cut side up, for 20 minutes. Keep warm until ready to serve.

Preparing the Steak

Dry the New York steaks and coat them with the Aloha Spice Prime Steak Seasoning & Rub. Firmly press the seasoning into the meat.

Cooking the Steak

Start the grill about 20 minutes into the roasting of the vegetables. When the grill is hot, brush the grating with the remaining 2 Tbsp. of olive oil. Set the steaks on the grill. Cook 3 to 4 minutes and turn a quarter turn to get the grill X marks. Turn the steaks over after a few more minutes. (Note: each grill is different and only you know how quickly the steak will cook on your grill).

To Serve

Place the steak on plate and surround with roasted vegetables and tomatoes. Garnish with chopped parsley. Enjoy!

Steak Fajitas & Tropical Salsa
(serves 2)

6 oz steak (a Tri-Tip steak is good for this dish)
3 Tbsp. Aloha Prime Steak Seasoning & Rub
4 Tbsp. olive oil
1 *each* red, yellow, green bell pepper & red onion cut in strips
4 flour tortillas
1/4 cup sour cream in a small bowl
Optional garnish: olives, chopped cilantro, avocado

Tropical Salsa
1 clove garlic, minced
2 cups diced tropical fruit (pineapple, papaya and/or mango)
1/4 cup small red onion, diced
2 stems green onion, chopped
1/2 red bell pepper, seeded and diced
2 Tbsp. cilantro, chopped
Juice of 2 limes
1/8 cup light rum *(optional)*
1 Tbsp. rice wine or cider vinegar
1 Tbsp. sugar (or to taste)
1 tsp. Alaea Red Hawaiian Sea Salt *(or other fine sea salt)*

Instructions for Steak Fajitas & Tropical Salsa

Preparing the Tropical Salsa
The Tropical Salsa can be prepared up to a day
in advance. Fold everything together, gently but
thoroughly. Take care not to crush the softer fruits.
Cover and refrigerate until ready to use.

Preparing the Steak
Slice the Tri-Tip across the grain, pat dry and season
thoroughly with the Aloha Prime Steak Seasoning & Rub.

Cooking the Fajitas

Heat a sauté pan or heavy cast iron skillet. Sauté the peppers and onion in 2 Tbsp. of olive oil for 3-4 minutes on high heat. Move the vegetables to the side, add the rest of the oil and quickly cook the steak.

To Serve

Set the vegetables next to the meat. Using tongs quickly heat the tortillas on the grill. Fold and arrange them with garnishes of olives, avocado, cilantro, sour cream and Tropical Salsa. Enjoy!

Aloha
Seafood
SEASONING & RUB

Aloha Seafood Seasoning & Rub

The soothing warmth of red pepper, balanced by garlic, fennel and some zesty lemon peel make this blend a perfect seasoning for almost any kind of seafood dish. Try rubbing it on a cut of fresh tuna for a great 'Ahi Burger, or a white fish such as sea bass for a delicious entree. Make a quick Italian Scampi by generously rubbing jumbo shrimp with Aloha Seafood Seasoning & Rub; sauté in olive oil and serve it with your favorite pasta.

Mahi~mahi & Salmon with Coconut Ginger Sauce

(serves 2)

6 oz. mahi-mahi filet (or other white fish)
6 oz. salmon filet
3 Tbsp. Aloha Seafood Seasoning & Rub
2 Tbsp. olive oil

Coconut Ginger Sauce
1/2 inch ginger root- peeled & finely minced
1 shallot – peeled & minced
2 Tbsp. sugar
1 cup coconut milk (canned or fresh)

Serve Fish With:
2 cups cooked jasmine rice
1/2 medium carrot - peeled and cut into julienne
8-10 snow peas - julienne
1/2 zucchini - julienne
1/2 trimmed red bell pepper - julienne

Garnish: Aloha Seafood Seasoning & Rub
6 slices lemon
2 Tbsp. pickled ginger *(optional)*
Chili oil & toasted shaved coconut *(optional)*

Instructions for Mahi & Salmon with Coconut Ginger Sauce

Preparing the Fish
Cut each filet of mahi-mahi and salmon filet in two pieces. Spread 3 Tbsp. Aloha Seafood Seasoning & Rub on a large plate. Lay the fish in the Aloha Seafood Seasoning & Rub: dredging (coating) each piece of fish with the spice mixture.

Coconut Ginger Sauce
Place the ginger, shallots and sugar with 3 Tbps. water in a saucepan and lightly brown. Remove from heat and carefully add the coconut milk. Return to heat and simmer. When it's thick enough for your liking- it's ready. Set it aside.

Cooking the Fish
Grill, Broil or Sauté the fish. If grilling, use the olive oil to lightly coat the grill. If broiling, drizzle a small amount of olive oil over the fish. If sautéing, use the olive oil to coat the pan.

The Vegetables

While the fish is cooking, steam the vegetables in a steamer basket. Keep warm until ready to plate.

To Serve

Set the vegetables on two warm plates, center the rice on top and lay one piece of mahi-mahi and one piece of salmon atop the rice. Ladle the Coconut Ginger Sauce around the vegetables and a small amount over the fish.

Garnish

The fish & sauce with a pinch of Aloha Seafood Seasoning & Rub. Drop a few small pools of chili oil in the sauce (optional). Arrange cut lemons, ribbons of pickled ginger and coconut shavings *(optional)*. Enjoy!

Shrimp & 'Ahi Wraps with Tropical Salsa
(serves 2)

8 - 16/20 prawns, cleaned, shelled and cut
6 oz. 'ahi tuna filet
4 Tbsp. Aloha Seafood Seasoning & Rub
2 Tbsp. olive oil
4 small flour tortillas
1/2 cup each shredded lettuce & cabbage
1/4 cup sour cream, 1/2 avocado

Tropical Salsa
1 clove garlic, minced
2 cups diced tropical fruit (pineapple, papaya &/or mango)
1/4 cup small red onion, diced
2 stems green onion, chopped
1/2 red bell pepper, seeded and diced
2 Tbsp. cilantro, chopped
Juice of 2 limes
1/8 cup light rum *(optional)*
1 Tbsp. rice wine or cider vinegar
1 Tbsp. sugar (or to taste)
1 tsp. 'Alaea Red Hawaiian Sea Salt *(or other fine sea salt)*

Instructions for Shrimp & 'Ahi Wraps with Tropical Salsa

Preparing the Tropical Salsa
The Tropical Salsa can be prepared up to a day
in advance. Fold everything together, gently but
thoroughly. Take care not to crush the softer fruits.
Cover and refrigerate until ready to use.

Preparing the Shrimp and Fish
Cut partway through the shrimp tails to make them
"butterfly". Spread 4 Tbsp. of Aloha Seafood Seasoning & Rub
onto a plate. Lay the shrimp & 'ahi into the seasoning,
coating them thoroughly.

Cooking the Fish
Grill, broil or sauté the shrimp & 'ahi. If grilling, use
the olive oil to lightly coat the grill. If broiling, drizzle
a small amount of olive oil over the 'ahi & shrimp. If
sautéing, use the olive oil to coat the pan. Please note:
the shrimp will cook faster than the 'ahi, so remove
them from the cooking surface and keep warm
until the 'ahi is ready.

To Serve

Divide the tortillas, lettuce, cabbage, sour cream and avocado between the two plates and add ramekins of the salsa to each. Fill tortillas with shrimp & 'ahi. Garnish with lime wedges *(optional)*. Enjoy!

Aloha Chicken & Pork

SEASONING & RUB

Aloha Chicken & Pork Seasoning & Rub

Our Chicken & Pork Seasoning & Rub reflects Hawaii's many cultures. The garlic and orange peel make it perfect for Pan Fried Chicken; just add 1 Tbsp. of seasoning to ¼ cup of flour, coat the chicken pieces and pan fry. Rub a chicken breast with the spice mixture and sear or grill it for a delicious Cajun Style Blackened Chicken. Use this blend to spice up a pork roast, coat generously before baking – delicious! Cube tenderloin for the grill, roll in Aloha Chicken & Pork Seasoning, skewer together with bell peppers and red onions for a Spanish Pork Skewer. The possibilities for how to use this blend are endless….!

Grilled Chicken Salad on Baby Greens
(serves 2)

2 - 6 oz. boneless, skinless chicken breasts
3 Tbsp. Aloha Chicken and Pork Seasoning
2 Tbsp. olive oil
Baby greens
Sliced avocado
Sliced tomato
Garnish with orange and lime slices

Tropical Vinaigrette
1 garlic clove, minced
1 Tbsp. red pickled ginger, minced
1/8 cup lime juice
1/8 cup pineapple or guava juice
1/8 cup rice wine vinegar
1/2 Tbsp. sesame oil
1/4 cup peanut oil
1 Tbsp. sugar
1 Tbsp. green onion, finely chopped
1/2 tsp. Aloha Chicken & Pork Seasoning & Rub

Instructions for Grilled Chicken Salad on Baby Greens

Tropical Fruit Vinaigrette
Combine all vinaigrette ingredients and whisk together
thoroughly.

Preparing the Chicken
Coat chicken with Aloha Chicken & Pork Seasoning & Rub.

Cooking the Chicken
Grill or Broil. Use the olive oil to lightly coat the grill.
If broiling, brush some olive oil over the chicken before
coating with the seasoning mix. To test for doneness,
lay the chicken on your cutting board and cut into the
side of the breast to give it a peek. It should be juicy,
but not pink. When done, set aside to cool.

Slicing the Chicken
Slice the breast cross grain - across the short side,
not down the length of the breast or it will be tough
to chew. Keep the chicken together in a tight pack to
make it easier to "fan" over the greens.

To Serve

Toss the greens with the tropical vinaigrette and arrange in center of plate. Fan the chicken breast slices over the greens. Garnish with tomato, avocado, orange & lime slices. Spoon a little vinaigrette over the chicken, avocado & tomato. Enjoy!

Pork Chops with Pineapple Relish *(serves 2)*

2 - 6 oz. pork chops
3 Tbsp. Aloha Chicken & Pork Seasoning & Rub
2 to 3 Tbsp. olive oil

Pineapple Relish
1/2 pineapple, peeled and cubed
1/4 cup raisins
1 onion, chopped
2 cloves garlic, minced
1/2 yellow or orange bell pepper, chopped
1 tsp. ginger, minced
1/2 cup cider or rice wine vinegar
1/2 cup sugar
1 tsp. cinnamon
1/2 tsp. turmeric *(optional)*
1 Tbsp. cornstarch dissolved in 1/8 cup of water

Serve with
Mashed sweet potatoes (purple if available)
1/2 cup broccoli florets
Garnish: sliced tomato, slice of lime *(optional)*

Instructions for Pork Chops with Pineapple Relish

Pineapple Relish
Mix and heat all ingredients (except the cornstarch and water) and simmer for an hour, stirring occasionally. Fold in the cornstarch and water mixture and return to a simmer for five minutes. Add a pinch of Aloha Chicken & Pork Seasoning & Rub to taste. Chill.

Preparing the Pork Chops
Dredge the chops in a plate of the Aloha Chicken & Pork Seasoning & Rub, coating them thoroughly.

Cooking the Pork Chops
Grill, broil or pan fry the chops. If grilling, use the olive oil to lightly coat the grill. If broiling, brush the olive oil over the chops before coating with the seasoning mix. If pan frying, use the olive oil to coat the pan.

The Vegetables

While the pineapple relish is simmering, cook and mash sweet potatoes. While the chops are grilling drop the trimmed broccoli into salted boiling water for 1 minute. Drain and keep warm.

To Serve

Arrange the broccoli next to the mashed potatoes. Lay the pork chops against the potatoes and garnish with the pineapple relish adding tomato slices & lime wedge *(optional)* to finish the plate. Enjoy!

Aloha Lu'au
BBQ
SEASONING & RUB

Aloha Lu'au BBQ Seasoning & Rub

The sweet, smoke flavor from tropical hardwood and Hawaiian 'Alaea Sea Salt are the main flavorings of food cooked *"Lu'au Style"* in an underground imu. The smoky, salty, slightly sweet flavor of Aloha Lu'au BBQ Seasoning & Rub is the perfect seasoning for anything you want to grill or BBQ. Or use it to add a delicious "cooked out of doors" flavor to your indoor cooking! Make a Jamaican style marinade by mixing 3 Tbsp. of spice blend with 3/4 cup of orange juice; marinade chicken pieces for 2-3 hours, then bake. It's also a great seasoning for homemade jerky.

Jumbo Shrimp & Chicken Tropical Kabobs
(serves 2)

8 oz. chicken breast, boneless, skinless, cut in 1½" pcs.
12 jumbo shrimp, peeled & "butterfly"
4 Tbsp. Aloha Lu'au BBQ Seasoning & Rub
8 cherry tomatoes
12 pieces of red or yellow bell pepper 1" in size
8 large pieces of red onion
8 pieces pineapple cubes approx. 1" in size
8 pieces zucchini cubes approx. 1" in size
3 Tbsp. olive oil
2 cups jasmine rice (or white rice)
8 metal skewers or bamboo skewers *(soak in water 1 hr.)*

Garnish
Pineapple wedges

Instructions for Shrimp & Chicken Tropical Kabobs

Preparing the Kabobs
Use 2 skewers for each kabob to keep the meat and vegetables from spinning when you turn them on the grill. A sturdy vegetable, like zucchini, should be used at each end. Spread the Aloha Lu'au Seasoning & Rub on a cutting board and roll the kabobs in the seasoning, making sure to coat the meat and shrimp thoroughly.

Grilling
Brush the grill with the oil. When grill is hot lay the skewers crosswise on it. Turn them often. The kabobs will be ready when the chicken is fully cooked.

To Serve

Place a scoop of rice on each plate. Set the skewers atop the rice. Garnish with pineapple wedges. Enjoy!

"Imu~Style" Chicken
(serves 2)

4 chicken thighs, boneless and skinless
2 Tbsp. Aloha Lu'au BBQ Seasoning & Rub
4 chard leaves, large (red or white)
4 pieces aluminum foil 6" x 8"
4 cut banana leaves, each measuring 6" x 12"
1 cup sweet potato and/or yams, peeled & chopped

Garnish (optional):
Pineapple wedges
Sliced papaya
Banana chips
Toasted coconut
Lime wedges
Baby salad greens

Instructions for "Imu-Style" Chicken

Preparing the Chicken
Coat the chicken with Aloha Lu'au BBQ Seasoning & Rub.
With the back of a chefs knife gently bruise the
surface of the chard stem with a light tap every 1/4"
or so. This will enable it to roll up easily without
breaking. Set the chicken thighs at the bottom of the
leaf and give it one full roll. Tuck up each side flap
and then roll over again and again if necessary. Place
each roll on the end of a banana leaf and roll in the
same manner. Now seal each in a piece of aluminum
foil – crimping shut the sides. See the following pages
for photos of preparing the chicken.

Cooking the Chicken

Set the chicken packages on a hot grill for 20 minutes. Turn after 10 minutes. Alternately, cook them in a 375° oven for 30 minutes. Meanwhile, either steam, boil, or bake the potatoes seasoning with a sprinkle of Aloha Lu'au BBQ Seasoning & Rub or 'Alaea Red Hawaiian Sea Salt.

To Serve

Carefully unwrap the foil. Watch out for the hot steam! The banana leaf can be removed and the chicken sliced to serve. Or plate the chicken leaving it in the banana leaf wrapping for each person to unwrap themselves. Place the potatoes near the chicken. Garnish with the salad greens, pineapple, papaya and lime wedges *(optional)*. Serve the banana chips and toasted coconut on the side *(optional)*. Enjoy!

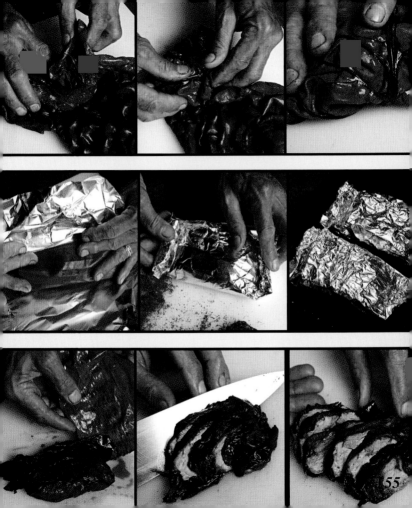

56

Aloha Spice Company

GOURMET SEA SALT

A Little Salt History

Salt has played an important role in our history. Before refrigeration, salt was one of the primary ways of preserving food. Salt played a prominent role in determining the location of great cities; many roads and trade routes were formed primarily for the transportation of salt. In ancient Rome, soldiers were sometimes paid their wages in salt (the English word *salary* is derived from the Latin *salarium* - payment in salt). The main sources for obtaining salt are evaporation of seawater and mining underground salt deposits. As a seasoning, sea salt is generally considered to be superior to rock salt. The Hawaiian Islands had numerous salt pans used by early Hawaiians to make salt, some of which are still in use today.

'Alaea Red Hawaiian Sea Salt

This salt is unique to the Hawaiian Islands. The red color comes from Hawaii's volcanic red clay ('Alaea). Rich in iron oxide and other trace minerals, 'Alaea Sea Salt is the traditional Hawaiian salt used to season and preserve foods. Historically, Hawaiians also used salt in ceremonies for cleansing, purifying and blessing.

'Alaea Salt is delicious on meat, chicken or fish. Use it as a rub or marinade. It is the authentic seasoning for Hawaiian dishes such as Kalua Pig and 'Ahi Poke. 'Alaea salt can be used as you would any other salt to give your dish a unique "flavor of the islands"!

Pele's Fire Aioli

1 clove garlic – finely chopped
1/4 cup olive oil
1 tsp. Pele's Fire Hawaiian Seasoned Salt
2/3 cup mayonnaise
3 or 4 tsp. lemon juice *(to taste)*

Directions

Blend garlic, olive oil & seasoning together. Drizzle
mixture into mayonnaise and whisk. Whisk in lemon juice
to taste. Serve on fish or crab cakes, as a vegetable dip or
in place of mayonnaise.

Oma'o Green Goddess Dressing or Dip

1/2 cup sour cream
1/3 cup mayonnaise
2 tsp. Oma'o Green Goddess Seasoned Salt
2 tsp. lemon juice *(or to taste)*
1 Tbsp. chopped fresh parsley *(optional)*

Directions

Blend seasoning with mayonnaise and sour cream. Whisk
in lemon juice to taste. Garnish with chopped parsley
(optional). Toss over salad greens, or use as a dip for
vegetables or chips.

Asian Gravlox with 'Alaea Red Hawaiian Sea Salt

1 side skinned salmon filet- about 2 or 3 pounds
1/2 cup minced peeled fresh ginger
6 Tbs. white sugar
8 Tbsp. 'Alaea Red Hawaiian Sea Salt
2 Tbsp. Aloha Seafood Seasoning & Rub
1/2 cup chopped cilantro
6 Tbsp. diced shallots
1/4 cup sake

Directions

Mix all the seasonings except the sake and spread over each side of the salmon. Wrap fish snuggly in a piece of cheesecloth. Place the fish into a baking pan and evenly splash the sake over each side of fish. Weight with another pan large enough to cover the length of the salmon and top with 2 or 3 large cans - bricks are traditionally used. Refrigerate for 2 or 3 days, turning the fish every 12 hours or so. It will feel firm to the touch when it's ready. Slice thinly and serve with toast points & lemon slice. Try a light casting of Black Lava Hawaiian Sea Salt as a garnish over the presented gravlox or a few sprigs of cilantro. Enjoy!

'Ahi Poke

6 oz. fresh 'ahi (yellow-fin tuna) cut in ¾" cubes
2 Tbsp. chopped Maui onion (or other sweet onion)
1 Tbsp. chopped green onion or fresh cilantro
1 Tbsp. soy sauce
1 tsp. toasted sesame seeds
1 tsp. 'Alaea Red Hawaiian Sea Salt (or to taste)
Pinch of Aloha Seafood Seasoning & Rub *(optional)*

Directions
Place 'ahi in a bowl and add other ingredients. Toss
mixture gently to blend evenly. Cover bowl and refrigerate
until well chilled, about 1 hour. Traditionally this is served
as a *'pupu'* (Hawaiian for 'appetizer'). Also try it atop
salad greens and chilled somen noodles (Japanese thin
noodles) for a delicious *Poke Salad*.

Note: Yellow-fin tuna is best for this recipe, but any
sashimi-grade fish can be substituted.

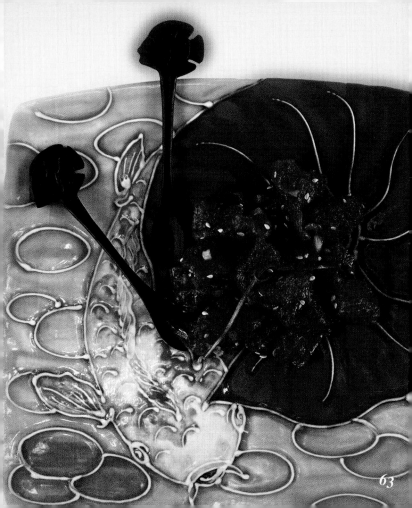

About Chef Michael Simpson

Chef Michael was born in Aberdeen, Washington. After receiving a BA in Art from Central Washington State University he expanded his artistic vision to food. In 1980 he completed a Professional Chef degree at the California Culinary Academy. He has over 30 years of culinary experience and now owns and operates *Chicolini*, a fine dining Private Chef service on the island of Kaua'i, Hawai'i. When he is not cooking he can be found surfing.

For more information contact:

Aloha Spice Company

Kaua'i, Hawai'i

www.alohaspice.com